About this book

Many children have difficulty puzzling out letters because they are abstract symbols. Letterland's worldwide success is all about its enduring characters who give these symbols life and stop them from being abstract. In this book we meet Impy Ink and Jumping Jim. Their stories are carefully designed to emphasise the sounds that the letters 'I' and 'J' make in words. This definitive, original story book is an instant collector's classic, making learning fun for a new generation of readers.

A TEMPLAR BOOK

This edition published in the UK in 2008 by Templar Publishing
an imprint of The Templar Company plc,
The Granary, North Street, Dorking, Surrey, RH4 1DN, UK
www.templarco.co.uk

First published by Hamlyn Publishing, 1985
Devised and produced by The Templar Company plc

ISBN 978-1-84011-785-1

Printed in China

Classic LETTERLAND Storybooks

Impy Ink's Invisible Ink

Also featuring
Jumping Jim in the Jungle

Written by
Lyn Wendon & Richard Carlisle

Illustrated by
Jane Launchbury

templar publishing

It was Monday morning.
Inside the Letterland Infant
School all the children were
working hard.

Some were listening to a story
about India.

Some were looking at pictures
of insects.

No one was interested in Impy Ink.

"Hmm," said Impy Ink to himself.
"I feel impish. I think I will play a trick."
So, while no one was watching, he
took a lemon and squeezed it into his
ink bottle.

Just then he heard the teacher say, "Let's invite all your mothers and fathers to a special Parents' Day at school. Do you think that's a good idea?"

"Yes! Yes!" said the children.

"Fill up your ink pens, then," she went on, "and write out a nice invitation."

So all the children dipped their pens into Impy Ink's bottle and started to write.

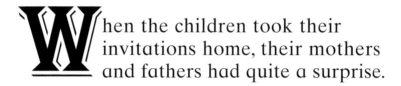

When the children took their invitations home, their mothers and fathers had quite a surprise.

There was nothing to be seen on the paper. All the writing had vanished.

"That's impossible!" the children cried. "We wrote the words ourselves!"

"Oh dear," said the teacher the next morning. "I think this must be one of Impy Ink's little tricks. Let's ask him if it is."

Impy Ink had a twinkle in his eye. "Yes," he confessed. "It was my special invention. It is called invisible ink. It makes the words you write disappear."

"But we need our parents to read our invitations!" the children cried.

"That's simple," laughed Impy Ink. "Just put the paper in the sunlight and wait a little while. The sun warms the invisible ink and makes it go brown. Then you can see the words again!"

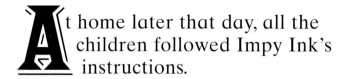

At home later that day, all the children followed Impy Ink's instructions.

Yes! When the ink turned brown in the sun, they could read the invitations.

Impy Ink's trick really worked!

"How did you do it?" said their mothers and fathers.

"It's just a little trick," said the children. They did not tell their parents about Impy Ink.

Instead they gave Impy Ink a big wink on Parents Day. Impy Ink gave them a big wink back.

Jumping Jim in the Jungle

Jumping Jim is Letterland's high jump champion. No one else can jump as high as he can.

One day Jim decided to try a new sport – parachute jumping.
So he went high up into the sky in a jet plane.

As he jumped out of the plane, a great wind caught his parachute. It was so strong, it carried him right out of Letterland!

"Jumping jelly beans!" shouted Jim. "This is the biggest jump I have ever made!"

The next moment Jim landed in the middle of a thick jungle. All around him were very tall trees. There were huge jungle flowers, and bushes so thick that they shut out the daylight like a blanket.

"What a wonderful jungle!" Jim said to himself, looking at all the amazing plants and flowers. "But how am I going to find my way out of it, back to Letterland?"

Just them Jim looked up into the trees. He saw a little furry animal. It was a jabber monkey, swinging by its tail.

Don't jump there!" cried the jabber monkey. "That's where the jaguar lives!"

"Jibber-jabber!" it shrieked.
"Jaguars can scratch and bite!"

Jim did not wait. He jumped right up beside the jabber monkey.

"Thank you for warning me," said Jim.
"By the way," he added, "do you know the way to Letterland?"

"I've never heard of it," replied the monkey. "But I can take you to a place where the jungle river joins the sea. Perhaps someone there will know."

"Come on, then!" said Jim.
So the monkey jumped on Jim's shoulder and they set off.

Jim and the jabber monkey jumped for many miles. Sometimes they just jogged for a change. Finally, they saw the sea.

A strange boat was tied up by the shore, "That's a junk from China," said the monkey.

"Jumping jellyfish!" cried Jim. "The captain must know where Letterland is."

"Can you tell me how to get back to Letterland?" Jim asked the captain of the junk.

"Letterland?" The captain shook his head. "There is no such place." "But I have just come from it," cried Jim.
"Then it will be on one of my maps," replied the captain.

So they looked through all the captain's maps. Letterland was not marked on any of them.
Finally, Jumping Jim spotted a tiny dot on one map that they had missed. He had to use a magnifying glass to read the name,

It said 'Letterland'! The captain looked very surprised.

"Maybe I can take you there," said the captain. "But my boat is very slow."

No, thanks. I think I'll jump it," replied Jim. "Jabber monkey, would you like to join me?"

"Jibber-jabber! Yes, please!" squeaked the monkey.

So the monkey grabbed Jim's jacket and off they jumped, all the way back to Letterland.

The captain watched them as far as his eyes could follow.
"I thought I'd seen everything," he said to himself, "but I have never seen a real live jumping letter. Letterland must be quite a jolly place! I think I will go there on my next journey."

THE END